UGLY SWEATY MEN
BECOME CEOs ALL THE TIME.
UGLY SWEATY WOMEN DON'T

Strive for equality!

Inga Beale

Nov 2022

MEN ARE JUDGED BY WHAT THEY CAN DO. WOMEN ARE STILL JUDGED FIRST BY THE WAY THEY LOOK. UGLY SWEATY MEN BECOME CEOS ALL THE TIME. UGLY SWEATY WOMEN DON'T.

First published in 2019 by Martin Firrell Company Ltd
10 Queen Street Place, London EC4R 1AG, United Kingdom.

ISBN 978-1-912622-12-2

Devised and edited by Martin Firrell.

Text is set in Baskerville, 11pt on 17pt.

Baskerville is a serif typeface designed in 1754 by John Baskerville (1706-1775) in Birmingham, England. Compared to earlier typeface designs, Baskerville increased the contrast between thick and thin strokes. Serifs were made sharper and more tapered, and the axis of rounded letters was placed in a more vertical position. The curved strokes were made more circular in shape, and the characters became more regular.

Baskerville is categorised as a transitional typeface between classical typefaces and high contrast modern faces. Of his own typeface, John Baskerville wrote, 'Having been an early admirer of the beauty of letters, I became insensibly desirous of contributing to the perfection of them. I formed to myself ideas of greater accuracy than had yet appeared, and had endeavoured to produce a set of types according to what I conceived to be their true proportion.'

INGA BEALE

Inga Beale was born in 1963, the second child of an English father and a Norwegian mother. She studied economics and accounting at Newbury College, Berkshire.

She began her career in 1982 at the Prudential Assurance Company in London where she trained as an underwriter, specialising in international treaty reinsurance.

She took a year away from work in 1989, cycling in Australia and backpacking in Asia.

She left Prudential in 1992 to work as an underwriter in the insurance division of General Electric. She joined GE's management in Kansas in 2001 and continued with GE Insurance Solutions, taking leadership roles in Paris and Munich.

In 2006 Inga became CEO of the Swiss reinsurance firm, Converium, transforming the company's financial performance. In 2008, she joined Zurich Insurance Group as a Group Management Board member.

The following year she was named the group's Global Chief Underwriting Officer. From 2012-13, she was the Group CEO at the privately held Lloyd's insurer Canopius.

She was announced as the new CEO of Lloyd's of London in December 2013, replacing Richard Ward. She served from 2014-2019 as the first female CEO in the insurance market's history.

Inga was the first woman and the first openly bisexual person to be named number one in the Financial Times power list of Leading LGBT+ executives. She was instrumental in the launch of Pride@Lloyds, an internal LGBT+ employee resource group, and has supported the LGBT+ Insurance Network.

In the 2017 New Year Honours list Inga was made Dame Commander of the Order of the British Empire (DBE) for services to the economy.

In June 2018 it was announced that she would be stepping down as CEO of Lloyd's after leading the global insurance and reinsurance market for five years. During her tenure she oversaw both technical modernisation and modernisation of the market's culture.

TRANSCRIPT

Inga Beale, CEO Lloyd's of London (2014-2019), in conversation with public artist Martin Firrell, 22 June 2018.

— Martin Firrell: **When did you first become aware that power existed in the world and operated, and you could either have, or not have, power?**

— **Inga Beale:** I think the first time I was really aware of power was when I was about ten, nine or ten. I played in the netball team at my school. I was very keen and I played in the position of wing defence. I was waiting, as usual, for the whistle to be blown so I could go into the centre. I was concentrating hard on the game. After that particular match, I was thrown out of the netball team. The teacher said to me, 'I don't like the way you were looking at me.' She felt I was being disrespectful but nothing could have been further from my mind. I was totally bemused. I was also deeply upset. I was very, very, very upset. I really couldn't work out what had happened. I thought, 'How could she think that I could have this sort of power or control? How could I, this little girl, be able to do that to the teacher?' Then of course I thought, 'But she has all the power. She's actually now throwing me out and I'm absolutely powerless. I want to get back into that team but I can't and yet she can't really explain what's happened.' I was embarrassed to try to explain it to my parents. I was embarrassed to say to them, 'It was the way I looked at her, and she threw me out.' I remember it being a quite distressing experience to me at that time.

— Did you have a sense of injustice as well?

— I think I did, yes. I mean it's difficult to remember everything that I felt at that time. But I just thought it was so unfair. I thought, 'What's happened here?!' All because of the way I looked at her.

— Do you have any sense of what she thought she saw in your expression?

— Yes I do because over my life I have had people commenting on the way I look. I even had it just the other day. I passed a homeless man in the street and he said, 'You know, everything is not that serious in life.' And I thought, 'Gosh, it's that damned look again.' I don't think women have ever said it to me but often I've had men say it. Sometimes workmen. I've walked past a building site and they've said, 'It's not the end of the world tomorrow.' There's something about my face even though I'm feeling fine. I've also had it from a boss of mine. This would have been about 15 or 16 years ago. He told me I had a sneer on my face when I spoke in management meetings, and it put him off, and it put others off. I thought, 'Gosh!' Then I really tried to change my facial expression when talking in meetings.

— Smile!

— Yes. I'm very aware of it. When I'm in a board meeting now, I try to sit there with a neutral expression. So, of course, now I get criticised because people can't read my expression and they can't work out what I'm really thinking. It's all very complicated. But the netball incident was the first time I remember thinking about power.

— **It's very strange isn't it, that people would comment on one's facial expression?**

— I've had this at the rugby club[1]. Half the team members would think I'm completely unapproachable and scary because of the way I look, and others think I look like the most friendly person on earth. I'm like Marmite.

— **That seems really strange to me. Before we met, I did my research and I looked at pictures of you and I saw you speak on videos and I thought you looked immensely approachable. And, of course, you were the only person who replied to me when I was asking people to join me in marking the 50th anniversary of the 1967 Sexual Offences Act[2]. Clearly you are approachable because you replied to me and got involved, so I don't understand.**

— My husband will say, 'Oh, that look. You've just got to do that slight glance in your eye and you have told everybody that you disapproved of what they've just said or done.' So that affects the way I try to hold my face, not so much in personal life but in business particularly.

— **People say that women are more scrutinised in positions of power about everything, don't they? What they look like. What they are wearing.**

— That's true. That's definitely true.

— **Do you think that's part of a broader patriarchal view that women are to be looked at in every aspect of life: daughters have to be pretty, brides are always glowing. The whole system is about the way women look but you don't have the same kind of language about the way men look.**

— You don't. Of course, in nature, it's often the other way round. The males of the species are really preening themselves. Go back some time ago and men were dressing gorgeously. Really, it was so important how they looked.

— **Wigs. Powder.**

— Mmmmm. All of this, and the flamboyance, and they could look just as beautiful. Something's happened, hasn't it? Over time it's changed. As a woman you do feel that you're completely under scrutiny. There's another thing too, though the majority of men don't notice this, I see ugly, sweaty men in positions of power: ugly faces, ugly features, ugly personalities and I think, 'They made it to that position but you would never get a woman who vaguely looked like that in the same job.'

— **Because women are so judged on appearance.**

— So judged.

— **Can I ask you about your journey from the netball team to being CEO of Lloyd's? What was that trajectory? How did you come to be CEO?**

— That's a long story. By the time I was ten, I was a little bit of a rebel. I was very much a loner. I was the middle child with two siblings. Both had blond hair. I had dark hair. They teased me that I was adopted. I used to go on long cycle rides. Even at seven I can remember cycling off on my own, being totally alone and never wanting to be around my brother and sister. I remember that and I remember hating my parents for bringing me into the world. Very, very young, at seven, I remember going into the kitchen and saying to my mother, 'I'm never getting married and I'm never going to have children.' I really resented my parents having me. As I got a bit older I would call them selfish: 'How could you be so selfish? It was always about you and what you wanted. How could you bring me into the world?' I was also pretty smart. At the time of the netball incident, I was having special maths classes. I was too advanced for the other pupils. I remember having a fight in the playground because there was a boy, Martin O'Hagan, I think his name was, and he said something rude and I said, 'Right, okay, we're going to have a fight.' We met at the school one evening. There were crowds of boys and crowds of girls and he ended up climbing onto the flat roof because he was so scared of me. He wouldn't come down and have a fight. That was what I was like at that age.

So nothing too bad. I didn't go around harming people. I was actually very well behaved but I had this streak in me. I was also very susceptible to kindness or acts of kindness. I can remember the headteacher saying, 'I'll give you fifty pence or ten pence (whatever it was in those days) if you jump the high jump five centimetres higher.' I did it and I got the money. He found a way of getting to me, this sort of slightly rebellious, slightly aggressive girl. Then I took my eleven plus and went to high school. I became very studious but I always remember an incident at the end of that first year. I got 97% in my French exam and another girl, Caroline (I can't remember her last name) got 98% and the French teacher said, in front of the whole class, 'Of course I'm very disappointed with Inga that she didn't get the top mark. Her father teaches French.' That just blew me away, so much so that from that day on, I became the rebel at the school. I was going to be the first girl to be caned. Ever! So, of course, I went round bragging that I was going to be caned. Then they couldn't cane me because they knew I was in it for the glory.

It just went on and on. I never played truant. I went to school every day but I was just quite aggressive. There was this little gang around me and I think we probably bullied a couple of the other girls, not physically but just by what we said.

I got thrown out of history class because the history teacher thought I was so unbearable. I used to have to go and sit in a room on my own. Again, I didn't think I was doing anything specific but she just found me really objectionable. I used to get detentions. It was a nice neighbourhood and a very nice school so we have to put this into perspective, but relative to the environment I was in, I was very difficult. My parents were going to send me off to boarding school at one time or to live with my lesbian aunts because they didn't know what else to do with me. I was very rude to my parents. I had a relationship with an adult male when I was only fourteen. So I was in an environment outside of school that was worldly. They were taking drugs. They were playing in a band. I used to play in a reggae band with them. I got through my exams at school not because I worked hard but because I was smart. If I didn't like a subject I would get zero and if I liked a subject, I would be good at it and I'd get top marks. It was just like that. I didn't want to work. Then I got threatened by the headmaster that I couldn't stay at school if I carried on like this. He thought this would make me behave and of course I just put two fingers up to him and said, 'Well, I'll go and do my A-levels at the local college then.' So I left school and went to the local college. You know, these threats didn't have any impact on me.

— **You seem to be very confident. Were you very confident back then?**

— It wasn't necessarily confidence.

— **Was it anger?**

— It was anger. At this time I was still very angry with my parents. Very angry. Still, you know, raging. Then I wanted to move from Newbury, which is a small town and come up to London. London was just so glamorous to me and I wanted to live here so I planned the move all on my own. I got a university place - well it was a polytechnic at the time - and I moved up to London. I found a little bedsit in Crouch End. Just totally on my own. I was eighteen. My family delivered me and my luggage, and then left, and for the first few months I didn't phone them once. I didn't contact them and I didn't go home. But I didn't like the course. I thought my fellow students seemed very young. I'd been mixing in an adult group so they all seemed like children to me and it was dull and boring.

I started in September and left by December. Then I needed a job. I didn't have any money so I just used to cycle around. I got an old bicycle and cycled around and found a job, ending up in insurance. I thought I might go back to university the next year because I wanted to be an architect then, or I thought I did at the time. But then I got engrossed in the City. It was all guys. All the people I worked with were men. Before long I was drinking pints of beer at lunchtime in The Lamb in Leadenhall Market. I got into this community which I sort of liked. I was one of the lads. I even went on one of their stag nights. I was just treated as a lad. But I was also having a relationship with a man at that time. I still had lots of anger. I had been working for about seven years in the City and we had a series of cocktail parties in the office because the cricket was on in the Caribbean. The office manager's wife worked for the Jamaican Tourist Board so she got all these posters advertising holidays in Jamaica. We plastered posters all around the office. We had goat curry and Red Stripe lager. Most of my colleagues were men. All the guests at the cocktail parties were men. That was all fine. The posters were a woman in a bikini, a woman in a bikini in a wet t-shirt, a woman in a wet t-shirt without a bikini. You know, that was it! These posters were left up on the office walls for weeks and weeks. Eventually I went to my manager on a Friday and I said, 'Look, I think I've been very patient, I think the posters should come down now.' And he said, 'Oh,

of course Inga. How could we have been so inconsiderate?'
I went home that night thinking, 'That's good.' I came in
early the following Monday morning. I used to get in early
because I was learning to touch-type. I don't really know why
but I decided that I needed to learn to touch-type. This was
in the Eighties. I was doing an evening class and I used to
come in early to practise on the keyboard. So I came in early
- nobody else was in the office - and walked round the corner,
and saw all the posters were down and thought, 'Fantastic!'
Then I turned the next corner and saw my desk was
completely wrapped up in the posters. I was just shocked. I
walked straight out and went home. And I thought, 'I'm
never working there again.' There were no mobile phones in
those days so my manager kept phoning my home, leaving
messages on my machine, and I refused to answer. Three days
went by. I eventually phoned him and said, 'Look, I'm not
coming back.'

I bought a round-the-world ticket. I didn't have any
money. I hadn't saved up any money. I'd already split up from
my boyfriend. I was renting a room in a house with a woman
I'd met at a yoga class. I didn't have anything, any ties. So I
just packed my rucksack, left the rest of my belongings with
a friend, got a round-the-world ticket and the next stop was
Bombay. I travelled around for a year, and ended up in

Australia where I got a job at the BBC working as a receptionist. At the time Michael Peschardt[3] was the correspondent in Australia. Part of my job was to send his tapes off to Tokyo because that was the only place with access to a satellite to beam them back to the UK. I remember Michael saying to me, 'I really think you could do another job, more than a receptionist. Have you ever thought about that?' Well, of course I'd been an underwriter in London but I didn't tell him any of that. I cleared up a backlog of mail left by my predecessor. There were about three tons of mail she'd never answered. I whipped through all of that. To cut a long story short, the manager at the BBC was a woman and I was so struck by her because she wore trousers to the office and here at Lloyd's women weren't allowed to wear trousers. Nobody referred to her gender. She was just the boss. I thought, 'Wow, this is really inspirational!' I thought, 'Maybe I can go back and maybe I can just be me.' So I came back to insurance and I said, 'I'm me.' I wore trousers. It had changed my life completely seeing this woman in that management role.

I started working for the insurance division of General Electric[4]. They had a proactive talent management programme which meant managers were required to promote women and people from ethnic minorities. I didn't know it at the time, but I was 'the woman', the one and only woman, and they were trying to promote me. But I said no to promotion.

— **Why did you say no?**

— I was petrified. I'd worked for 14 years by this stage but never managed a person in my life and didn't think I was capable of it.

— **I suppose it doesn't match with the seven-year-old riding the bicycle alone.**

— That's what I mean. In a way, I didn't have any confidence. I had confidence enough to get on a plane and go around the world and have all sorts of things happen to me as a woman travelling through India on her own in the 1980s. But confidence at work, I had none. I really didn't. So it was very interesting. I went on a week-long assertiveness course for women. There were eight women on the course and it had a very powerful impact on me. It helped me understand how other people saw me and I came back to the office and I said, 'Okay, I'll take the promotion.' That was my first role in management, first company car, you know, it was all very exciting. Then I started to understand how satisfying it could be to manage other people and develop them and see them be successful. I started to enjoy that and I took opportunity after opportunity that GE put in front of me. Now if I hadn't worked for GE, if I'd got perhaps any other job in the London market, I don't believe I would have become CEO of Lloyd's. Their talent management programme supporting women and people from ethnic minorities made such a difference for me.

— **Very forward looking.**

— Then I got offered an opportunity to go to the US, which I took, got exposure to all the big bosses there, and managed to impress them. I went to Paris and I ran all of continental Europe from Paris then I got the next promotion which was one in EMEA - Europe, Middle East and Africa. I moved to Munich. I was the CEO of this major business. But again, all within GE because they absolutely supported any type of minority. Then GE sold its business to Swiss Re and at the same time I was being headhunted: would I take a CEO role at a Swiss company that was in dire trouble? It was a reinsurance company that had been spun off from the Zurich Insurance Group in 2001. This was now 2005. It had lost a lot of money. It had been downgraded[5]. It was a disaster. And they couldn't find a CEO to take the job. They had been searching for a year. Staying at Swiss Re was an option or I could take this new opportunity and I thought, 'Well, what have I got to lose?' So I said, 'Oh this sounds all right'. GE didn't pay very much so I got a big increase in salary and it was a lot of money for me. I moved to Switzerland and took over as the CEO of this company in trouble. I didn't understand what I was taking on. I'd never run a plc in my life. I didn't realise that I would be the first female ever to run a financial services institution in Switzerland. I was 44 or 45 at the time. In Switzerland they thought that was incredibly young. I was British. They had done their research and found out I had played rugby, so it was 'Inga the Winger'! This extraordinary British woman has appeared out of the blue! I became an intriguing person in the Swiss media. I was constantly being written about but in an incredibly supportive way. Looking back, it was all incredibly supportive. I was naïve. I went in. I just wanted to turn the company around and I had no ego. I was nice to the people in the media. I respected them. A journalist would come in and I would say, 'Oh, have a seat. Do you want a coffee?' And I'd just chat to them because that's me. And I think they were so struck by this - it just wasn't their style - that I became this intriguing thing for them. I got great positive support from the media in Switzerland. We turned the company around and most of the shareholders were happy. We doubled the market capitalisation. Everything was rosy and it was wonderful. I couldn't have been more happy and I felt that I had nurtured this baby back to health.

Then a hostile bid came along from a French company. I went down to what I thought was rock bottom. I was not married at that time but I had been in a relationship with a woman. I'd moved to the US with her. I'd taken her with me secretly because I wasn't out at work. She'd had to give up her job. She was on a student visa. She had to go to university every day because we couldn't go in and out of the country without her having a proper academic record. She had moved with me from London to the US, from the US to France, to Germany, to Switzerland. She had been with me all the time. And I still wasn't out at work. So that was all going on in the background. I heard about this hostile takeover bid over dinner. A major shareholder had combined forces with a French company and we believed this company had done something illegal under Swiss regulations. But they joined forces and they were in such a strong position together that they were going to have almost complete power to take over the company. This major shareholder had invited me to a big dinner. He was an asset manager and he had about a hundred guests. They were all people he invested money for. I sat next to him at dinner and he was charming and lovely. At the end of the dinner he said, 'Inga before you go...' and he told me he was combining with another shareholder to take over the company. I said, 'Well, I'm very disappointed. I thought you had faith in me to run the company.' He said, 'Oh, we want you to stay.'

It was about a half hour drive back home. My girlfriend was there and it was about half past midnight on a Friday night. I had never been hysterical in my life, and I was hysterical. In other words, I was screaming, crying. My world had, as far as I was concerned, completely gone. It had been taken away from me, my entire life. I couldn't see a future. I didn't sleep. My girlfriend was worried because she'd never seen me like that. I'd always been so strong and always had everything under control. I had to be in the office by nine the next morning because we'd called a meeting of the whole board. I was never hysterical again and I never shed another tear over work, after that night. I learned that we are just pawns in this world. It doesn't matter how good you think you are as an individual. If you cannot manage the politics, if you don't really know what's going on, you are immaterial to the financial markets. You are nothing. Nothing.

— **It's a tough lesson though. The picture you paint is of a very young and empassioned person, albeit with a lot of anger. You go through this journey and really commit to something, and it's a real kick in the shins, isn't it? Then to have to reevaluate your relationship with the whole thing and step back. It's**

26

quite dramatic.

— It was very, very dramatic. And of course, we'd moved. Our whole life was set up in Switzerland and it just seemed that everything was uncertain.

— **What actually happened with the takeover? Did you exit yourself from that whole situation?**

— We fought for months because we decided we wanted to stay independent. I had been brought in by the board to turn this business around and none of us wanted to be subsumed into this hostile company. We fought and fought and fought and fought. It was the first hostile takeover ever in the world of reinsurance. Historically it had been all so pally and clubby. Eventually we realised that they had so much control over the shareholder base that we had to submit. During that time we managed to increase their offer so the shareholders were all going to be happy, and ultimately the board has to act in the interests of the shareholders.

So we made the decision and we held a special general meeting. Swiss television were all over us so we had to learn to do live television for the first time ever. I remember we brought in a media company straightaway to help me and the Chief Financial Officer. We had this training which lasted about three-quarters of a day. And all for live television.

— **Were you nervous?**

— I think I probably was incredibly nervous but you had to do it because you had to be strong in front of all of these people: all your clients, all your employees. We held the Special General Meeting. Swiss TV reported it. It was just amazing. I was asked to stay on as the Deputy CEO but I said, 'What's a deputy CEO? That's nothing!' So I chose to leave. I was offered several jobs but the one I took was at Zurich Insurance. I took that really because a) we could stay in Switzerland and b) I was totally inspired by the boss. He was a guy called Jim Schiro[6], a New York Italian accountant, who had been brought in from the consulting firm Price Waterhouse Coopers to save the Zurich Group. He had succeeded in turning its fortunes around. He was amazing. And he persuaded me to take the job. He retired after about two and a half years. I knew that was on the cards. When his successor was appointed, I was very happy because it was the Chief Investment Officer who had welcomed me with open arms when I first joined the company. I thought, 'Oh, this is a nice guy. I totally respect him.' But then the culture started to change and I thought, 'He doesn't need me. He doesn't need a change agent.' It was a very amicable departure.

My PA at the Zurich Group said to me, 'Inga you need a CEO job. You're fine in the Executive Committee reporting to the CEO but I saw you as a different person when you were running Converium. I think you need to be a CEO.' So then I set out to get a CEO job. I got offered the CEO of Canopius here in Lloyd's. I'd got married to my girlfriend but she left me for a younger woman. It all happened at about the same time. I went into, not hysteria as before, but into a deep, deep depression. I would do a bottle of vodka a day easily. Didn't get out of bed. I thought my life was over. She'd left and it was just awful and if it wasn't for my friends I don't know how I would have got through that. But my typical style is to get up and fix things, so I said, 'Right, we're divorcing. Now.' Under Swiss law she was entitled to 50% of everything. We sold property. I had to remortgage. I had to pay her 50% of everything.

When I got offered the job here in London, I was thinking, 'New life. I'll go back to London. I'll start again.' But then I met Philippe, who's my husband now, and I thought, 'Well, maybe I won't make the decision to move to London just now. I'll keep my apartment in Zurich and see how it goes.' For four years I commuted between Zurich and London until two and a half years ago when I said, 'I can't do the commuting any more.' I said to Philippe, 'After 36 years in Zurich, would you be prepared to move to London?' And he said, 'Yes!' We moved to London and I stopped flying from City Airport every week which was actually a really nice relief. After two years at Canopius, we sold the company to a Japanese firm. It meant it was time for me to exit because I didn't want to run a division of a big group. I decided to leave and the job of CEO came up at Lloyd's. So here I am nearly five years later.

— **Can I ask you about the assertiveness training you talked about? You said the training was helpful in large part because you were able to see how others saw you. Was that the aspect of the course of most benefit - understanding how you were coming across rather than assertiveness itself?**

— That's the piece I remember.

— **I've heard a few things about assertiveness training and a few feminist voices saying, 'Why should we have to become more assertive? Rather than training women to be more assertive, why not train men to be less aggressive?' I can see both sides of the argument. Why should women have to modify themselves? Equally, practically, if you want to operate in a tough environment you're going to need some tools to help you. I was really struck that you said it was your sense of how others saw you that had the greatest impact. That's different from learning to assert yourself, isn't it?**

— It's completely different. About 80% of that week involved teaching us how to be assertive in meetings. I don't really remember any of that. I remember there was an exercise where we had to make a collage of cutout images to illustrate how we saw ourselves. We made the collage on our own, then got together, first in pairs and then in a group, to discuss how we saw each other. It was deeply emotional. People were sobbing because we were going really deep. I had painted myself as this ice maiden. I was this absolutely impenetrable ice maiden and the people around me said, 'No, we don't see you like that at all!' We discussed how people perceived me and I talked about my lack of confidence. They said, 'But you come over so confidently!' And I said, 'But do I?' It seems so simple and primitive. In some ways, I am like an ice maiden. I'm told I'm not very deep and sensitive. And I'm not sensitive: I throw everything away. I don't keep things for sentimental reasons. It's my coping mechanism. I don't keep things and I'm not very sentimental.

— **But they're different things: being sentimental and being sensitive.**

— That's what I remember about the course. It was more about me learning about the difference between the way I saw myself and the way others saw me. That course also gave me the courage to dress differently. Again it sounds like such a simple thing but they looked at what colours were best for you. I completely changed my wardrobe and I suddenly felt confident. I even walk differently. It was amazing. But it doesn't work for everyone. I said to a colleague, 'Why don't you do this course, it was just incredible?' She went but it didn't change anything for her. It had no impact on her whatsoever even though it was exactly the same course. I don't remember the assertiveness bit. I just remember this reflection on me and somehow coming out with this radiant feeling of confidence.

— **I think that's very powerful. If you think you're not coming across as particularly confident then that can make it worse, of course. It's a vicious circle. I also think there's something very interesting in the subtle difference between sentimentality and sensitivity. The story you've just described really is incredibly emotional.**

— Yes it is.

— **Can I ask you about being part of the LGBT+ community? Obviously you've done things that are very valuable: 1) being a woman and running things so other women can see it's possible and 2) being an out bisexual person, which is a very personal and private thing made into a public thing. I think that**

kind of visibility is a benefit to all people, not necessarily just LGBT+ people. When people come into contact with someone who is living authentically, it frees them to be authentic. But that must have taken a degree of courage, mustn't it?

— Yes, certainly when I came out officially at work. I was always out in my non-work life. In fact, before I went travelling, I had been in this long term relationship with a guy. When that broke up, I moved in with the woman I'd met at yoga. I remember bumping into my sister that day. I had been crying and I said, 'Oh, it's because Adrian and I are splitting up. Don't tell mum and dad. I'm going to tell them tomorrow.' I was going down to see them, and he was going off to see his parents. Anyway, my sister can't keep her mouth shut and she'd obviously told my parents because I got a phone call from my father before I had even left home to see them. He said, 'It's absolutely fine. You can move in with a woman.There's no problem with you being a lesbian.' I thought, 'I'm not a lesbian!' I thought, 'I'm just leaving my boyfriend and staying with the woman I've met at yoga.' But because my father's sister lived with a woman in a lesbian relationship for 50 years, that's what he assumed. This was several years before I ever had a relationship with a woman. So you see, in a way, I was always out. At home there was no problem but at work it was more of a challenge. I eventually came out because of one incident in particular. At the time of the hostile takeover bid, I had a wonderful PA. She was fabulous. We got on so well. After the hostile bid, we both left the firm. She took me out to dinner on a Saturday night because she felt sorry for me, thinking I was on my own. She didn't know anything about the existence of my girlfriend. She asked me how I was coping with everything and I thought, 'I've deceived this woman. This is absurd. Here I am on a Saturday night. My girlfriend should be here. This is the most ridiculous and bizarre situation.' And from that day on I said, 'I'm not doing this any more!' That was actually the trigger point. My PA is now a dear friend, Sheila. It was that dinner with her. I remember the restaurant. I remember what we ate. I remember everything. And I said, 'Right, no more!' I went to the Zurich interview and I told the CEO upfront, 'I'm with a woman, I hope that doesn't cause a problem.' And he said, 'No.' Why the hell had I been quiet about it for all these years? I mean, how ridiculous is that? So that was how I came out. When I came to Lloyd's, I was approached to join the FT list of influential LGBT+ execs. I had only been here a few months and I said, 'No, I can't risk it'. For the first year I wasn't really talking openly in the media. I thought, 'I can't do it, I have to focus on my job,

I have to get the respect of the market.' It wasn't until a year later that I felt able to say, 'Okay, I'll do it!' But that took a lot of courage and we discussed within Lloyd's whether or not I should put my name up for it.

— **And was the mood supportive at Lloyd's, Or very cautious?**

— Well, my comms team were absolutely supportive. I was incredibly nervous about telling my chairman. He knew my sexual history but it was another thing entirely for it to appear in the FT and be read in Dubai and wherever, so we managed it as carefully as we could.

— **Which is the right thing to do.**

— But I did get hate mail. Letters cut out and glued to pieces of paper, and emails, and other letters from the US, telling me I didn't deserve to be alive. Oh yes, I got all of that.

— **I find that shocking.**

— I haven't had anything like that for the past two years but, yes, I got all of that.

— **Did you ignore it all, send it all to the police?**

— No, I ignored it. With hindsight, I think, 'Why didn't I keep it? I would have it all now.' Again it's my mechanism for coping. Get it all out. So if an abusive email comes in, I just delete it. Or I open a letter and I start reading it and if it's abusive, I just throw it away. It's my way. Moving on.

— When we did the 1967 work, I got all kinds of emails. One said I was disgraceful because I wasn't acknowledging how hard men had worked for the last hundred years to create the fair and open society we enjoy today. It was nothing to do with LGBT+ activists or the feminist movement or the Pankhursts. Nothing! It was all about men who had worked really hard. One thing I really object to is our words being twisted. A group in America said of my 1967 artwork, 'This isn't about LGBT+ equality. It's not about acknowledging the 50th anniversary of the 1967 Sexual Offences Act, it's the progressives co-opting the LGBT+ story to destroy America and the American family, and traditional, normal ways of life.' It's alarming when people are so delusional that they believe this kind of nonsense. I had a letter from a man saying, 'I'm going to contact everyone who has ever been associated with you.' He listed out all these companies that had sponsored our work in the past. He was going to write to each one telling them our work was dangerous rubbish. And I thought to myself, 'Good luck with that because we find it hard enough to get in touch with them ourselves!' It can be funny but it's also very destructive.

— I don't think we should underestimate the power of things like the FT list of influential LGBT+ executives because it gives LGBT+ people credibility in the business community. How can somebody now really criticise me? I met the editor of the FT right at the beginning and I am really thankful to her for having the courage to publish the list. It's very difficult to criticise now.

— **When I was making the 1967 work, I went through the entire FT power list of 100 LGBT+ people. I wrote to everyone who offered an email address, about 60 people in total, and only two people replied. One was you and the other was Antonia Belcher[7].**

— Oh yes, I know, Antonia. She's lovely.

— **It struck me that only women wrote back to me. I was writing about a really significant milestone for gay men and none of the gay men wrote back.**

— [Laughter]

— **I'm interested in the idea of power and what it means to women. I have the sense that women tend to disconnect power from aggression. I think a lot of power is about imposition and domination but I think women use power in ways which are much more about knowledge and influence. I don't think**

women necessarily feel the need to be right or to impose a view. This, in turn, suggests to me a kind of openness, which might explain why the only people who wrote back to me were women even though one would hope that gay men would have a little more insight and intuition about other ways of being powerful.

— I talk about this a lot to Shirine, my Chief Operating Officer. I brought her in to modernise the market from a technology point of view. We are the ones making this modernisation happen but we never take the headlines. We don't need to. We just make it all happen behind the scenes. We laugh about it. We say, 'We've got all the power here, we're making it all happen, but it's better if the men have the kudos. It's better if they take ownership of the modernisation because then they'll embrace it.' For us the modernisation will mean a) we'll succeed and b) it will pave the way for the next big fantastic opportunity for us. We don't need to be out there saying, 'Yes, it was me.'

— **But that's a very global view, isn't it, a view that's disconnected from the personal ego? I've heard it said again and again that men always need to be identified with success, with achievement. I heard about a man who always introduces himself as the**

Chief Executive of such-and-such, but never actually says what his name is. He just tells people how powerful and important he is.

— How funny.

— **And I think there's a globalness, a wideness of perspective as well, about the scenario you're describing with Shirine.**

— When I meet people, I nearly always give my role because otherwise they'll just dismiss you as unimportant. So that's what I do. If I'm at a City gathering or whatever, I always give my name and I say what my role is, and then you've got the interest. Otherwise you're just another woman who, probably in their eyes, doesn't have any importance.

— **I'm interested by the idea of gender being connected with an estimate of someone's worth or significance. There's a strand of French feminism from the 1970s[8] that described gender politics as a question of citizenship. In this view, gender equates with a level of citizenship. The primary form of citizenship is gendered male and the second-class form of citizenship is gendered female. If you view gender through that lens, suddenly you realise the truth that there are two forms of citizenship available. That shows up gender inequality in stark** outline and makes one angry because, in this model, women are automatically regarded as less important, as second class. I have heard stories about very successful women being ask to make the tea because the assumption is that any woman present must be there to fulfil that role. As a corrective, women have to keep stating, 'I am this!'

— Yes!

— We are all born on the tilted ground of gender inequality: men run everything. Because we're born on this tilted ground, it appears flat to us. We've never known anything different. I think that's what you perceive when you have to give your title to avoid the assumption that you're a woman and you don't matter. Actually that is true. That's the world we live in. If you're a woman you don't matter or if you're gay you don't matter. I think getting the idea that the ground is not level into the public consciousness is really important. I also hear women say, 'We need to do things to promote the cause of women.' But it's always within the context of accepting the tilt of the ground. I think we need to step back and say, 'This inclination of the ground in favour of the male citizen is a fundamental flaw!' We need to call it out

and change it! Men run everything. They may say, 'Come on little lady, come and play the game with us!' But they never say, 'Come and change the game!' And very few men say, 'Let's share the game.' The implication for women is always, 'You've made it over the threshold. You can come and sit in the corner and do bits and bobs but don't upset the status quo.' Ultimately, the future will have to be about upsetting the status quo, about making the ground level.

— Do you think there's anything to do with physical strength in this? I say that because I can remember we used to play a game at primary school called British Bulldog. We used to play rounders too. For those games you'd have somebody picking the team and I was always picked. The boys would pick me because I was physically quite strong and tough. I do sometimes wonder if that has an impact, particularly when you're young. Maybe the impact continues further on in life. Whenever I see a woman getting up on stage to give a presentation, I feel nervous for her. I think, 'Oh, do well, do well.' If I saw a women who's tall and striking, I would have fewer doubts. If I see a small woman, physically small, getting up, I feel almost more nervous for her. I'm already being impacted by her physical stature. If boys are physically stronger at certain times, that must have an impact on girls when they see that men have this particular power. I was just about the only girl who was always picked to be on that team for Bulldog or rounders simply because I was physically very strong.

— **I think it runs very deep although it becomes less and less relevant, of course, as success is based on ideas.**

— It does!

— **Physical prowess becomes less important as success is based on influence or emotional intelligence, which is becoming more and more important and understood to be so.**

— But that's only when we get to be grown-ups, when we're more serious and knowledgeable.

— **The fact of a difference in physical strength is brought home when we're young but may then have a lasting influence in later life.**

— That's right.

— **This seems like a good time to talk about Olympe de Gouges and her Declaration of the Rights of Woman. I think she was incredibly practical and logical in her observations. For example, she made the observation that in nature you don't see the male**

of the species automatically in charge. She also suggested that if women have to pay tax, they need to have an equal voice and representation. If women are required to contribute economically then they need to be able to compete economically. She's very practical. She makes the point that women supported men who were oppressed before the French revolution. Post revolution, if the men are no longer oppressed where does that leave women? Are they to remain as second-class citizens? If so, it's no revolution at all. Women need to be part of the revolution. I found her so modern.

— The question is, how can we get to this lovely equal state? I do think we are fighting against inequality all the time. I am always trying to think about equality. I just think, 'Fair, equal. Fair and equal. Balance. Balanced.' These are the words I try to hold in my head constantly. I think this is what Olympe de Gouges is trying to get to. But we have so much talk that's polarising. We have a dinner club for LGBT+ senior leaders in insurance. We get together every now and then, and one of the topics of conversation at the last dinner related to shared parental leave. A firm had introduced equal parental leave and received feedback from the female members of staff that said, 'Why are you helping the privileged man even more?' There was this anger coming through from some of the women saying, 'Men already have all the perks and benefits and now you're giving them what we have!' It's more equal but they were resenting it. This is why it's all so complicated isn't it? It was just one example. I thought. 'No, we have to strive for this, we have to strive for equality.' We have to try and take these gender-related words and ideas out of the equation. We have to support equal benefit for all regardless of gender. That's what really struck me about this. The answer as to how we achieve full equality is very elusive. It just seems overwhelming, too big an issue to address. But we have to try. We have to aim for it. Even in the context of Lloyd's, I was constantly trying to challenge everything we were writing as policy or practice. Let's make sure we're just being absolutely equal. That's our challenge especially when you're starting from a very unequal place.

OLYMPE DE GOUGES

Olympe de Gouges (7 May 1748 - 3 November 1793), born Marie Gouze, was a French playwright and political activist whose writings on women's rights and the abolition of slavery reached a wide audience.

She began her career as a playwright in the early 1780s. As political tensions rose in France, she became increasingly politically engaged. She became an outspoken opponent of the slave trade in the French colonies and she began writing and publishing political pamphlets and posters. Today she is perhaps best known as a proto feminist and early women's rights advocate who demanded that French women be given the same rights as French men.

In her *Declaration of the Rights of Woman and the Female Citizen* of 1791, she questioned the assumption of male authority and challenged gender inequality head on. She was executed by guillotine during the Reign of Terror[9] for attacking the regime of the revolutionary government and for her association with the Girondists[10].

Marie Gouze was born in 1748 into a petit bourgeois family in Montauban, Quercy in the present-day department of Tarn-et-Garonne, southwestern France. She was married off, at the age of 16, to Louis Aubry, a caterer. The marriage took place in 1765 against her will. In her semi-autobiographical novel *Mémoire de Madame de*

Valmont contre la famille de Flaucourt she wrote, 'I was married to a man I did not love and who was neither rich nor well-born. I was sacrificed for no reason that could make up for the repugnance I felt for this man.' Her husband died a year after they were married and, in 1770, she moved to Paris with her son to live with her sister. She never married again, calling the institution of marriage 'the tomb of trust and love'.

In 1788, she published *Réflexions sur les hommes nègres*, demanding compassion for the plight of slaves in the French colonies. She came to the public's attention with the play *l'Esclavage des noirs (Black Slavery)* staged at the Comédie Française[11] in 1785. Her anti-slavery arguments brought her criticism and threats and she was also attacked simply because she was a working woman. The actor Abraham-Joseph Bénard[12] remarked, 'Mme de Gouges is one of those women to whom one feels like giving razor blades as a present, who through their pretensions, lose the charming qualities of their sex... Every woman author is in a false position, regardless of her talent.'

Olympe de Gouges was defiant. She wrote, 'I'm determined to be a success, and I'll do it in spite of my enemies.' The pro-slavery lobby mounted a press campaign against her play and she eventually took legal action, forcing the Comédie Française to stage *l'Esclavage des noirs*. The play closed after only three performances because the lobby had paid hecklers to sabotage the run.

She regarded the prospect of the French Revolution with optimism, but soon became disenchanted when the revolution's call for equality did not extend to women. In 1791, She became a member of Les Amis de la Verité[13] (The Society of the Friends of Truth), an association pursuing equal political and legal rights for women. Members sometimes gathered at the home of the well-known women's rights advocate, Sophie de Condorcet.[14] Here, for the first time, Olympe de Gouges expressed her famous maxim:

'A woman has the right to mount the scaffold to be hanged. She must equally have the right to mount the speaker's platform to be heard.'

The *Déclaration des droits de l'homme et du citoyen* (*The Declaration of the Rights of Man and of the Citizen*) was adopted by France's National Constituent Assembly in 1789. The Declaration holds the rights of man to be universal. It was a core statement of the values of the French revolution and became the basis for a nation of free men protected equally by the law.

In response, Olympe de Gouges wrote the *Déclaration des droits de la femme et de la citoyenne* (*Declaration of the Rights of Woman and the Female Citizen*) followed by *Contrat Social* (*Social Contract*) which proposed that the institution of marriage should be based on strict equality between the sexes.

As the revolution progressed, she became more and more vehement in her writings. Her poster *Les trois urnes, ou le salut de la patrie, par un voyageur aérien* (*The Three Urns, or the Salvation of the Fatherland, by an Aerial Traveller*) led to her arrest in 1793. *Les trois urnes* proposed that the public should be given the opportunity to choose one of three forms of government: the first option, a unitary republic, the second, a federalist government, or the third option, a constitutional monarchy.

At her trial, the presiding judge denied Olympe de Gouges her legal right to a lawyer on the grounds that she was more than capable of representing herself.

On 3 November 1793 the Jacobins[15] sentenced her to death and executed her for seditious behaviour and for attempting to reinstate the monarchy. Her body was laid to rest in the cemetery of the Madeleine.[16] Olympe's last moments are described in a journal kept by an anonymous Parisian: 'Yesterday, at seven o'clock in the evening, a most extraordinary person called Olympe de Gouges, who held the imposing title of woman of letters, was taken to the scaffold, while all of Paris, though admiring her beauty, knew she didn't know her limitations... She approached the scaffold with a calm and serene expression on her face, and forced the furies of the guillotine,[17] which had driven her to this place of torture, to admit that such courage and beauty had never been seen before... That woman... had thrown herself into the revolution, body and soul. But having quickly perceived how atrocious the system adopted by the Jacobins was, she chose to retrace her steps. She attempted to unmask the villains through the literary works that she had printed and displayed in public. They never forgave her, and she paid for her carelessness with her head.'

LETTER TO THE QUEEN OF FRANCE

Olympe de Gouges, 1791

Madame,[18]

I am not used to addressing royalty so I dedicate this text to you without the ingratiating tone so often used by courtiers. I simply want to speak to you freely. I could have waited for more liberal times, but I'm determined to speak freely now even though I may be punished for it.

When the entire French Empire accused you of causing its misfortunes, only I had the courage to defend you in such terribly difficult times. I could never believe that a princess raised in the French nobility could be capable of that kind of viciousness.

Yes, Madame, when I saw people turn against you I wrote in your defence. Now I can see that the majority of your critics are closely watched and will not act because they are afraid of the legal consequences. So now I will say, Madame, things I would not have said before.

If war comes to France, I will no longer consider you a falsely-accused Queen. I will feel for you, but regard you as an enemy of the French people. Remember, Madame, that you are a mother and a wife. Use your influence to encourage the princes to return to France. If you use your influence wisely it will strengthen the monarchy for generations to come and mend your relationship with France. Using your influence in this way is the real duty of any Queen. Any involvement with political intrigue, factions and violent plans would bring about your downfall, if it seemed reasonable to suspect you of those things.

Instead, Madame, associate yourself with the nobler cause of the Rights of Woman. The support of someone in your position would transform the cause of equality. If you were less enlightened, Madame, I'd be concerned that you might put your own interests before the cause of women's equality. Think about your legacy. The worst crimes are always remembered and so are the greatest achievements. But they're treated very differently by history. Great achievements are held up as examples for others to follow. The worst crimes are remembered as curses on humanity.

You will never be criticised for working to improve society or for encouraging women to have the strength to demand justice. Unfortunately for the new government, equality isn't something that can be achieved in a day. The revolution will only be complete when all women are aware of the injustice they face because of their gender. Madame, support this great cause. Defend the rights of women and soon you will have one half of France on your side and at least a third of the other half.

These, Madame, are the goals you should pursue and take credit for. Believe me, Madame, life is brief, especially a Queen's, if that life is not characterised by love for the people and acts of selfless generosity.

Is it true that some Frenchmen are arming foreign powers against their own country? Why would they do that? For superficial privileges, for illusions. Believe me, Madame, I predict the monarchist party will destroy itself. It will abandon tyranny and everybody will rally to defend France.

These, Madame, are my principles. In speaking to you about France, I have lost track of the point of this dedication which shows how all good Citizens place the interests of their country above their personal interests.

With the deepest respect,

Madame,

I am your very humble, and very obedient servant,

de Gouges

DECLARATION OF THE RIGHTS OF WOMAN AND THE FEMALE CITIZEN

Olympe de Gouges, 1791

Are men capable of being fair and reasonable? This question is asked by a woman. As a woman, I have the right to freedom of speech if nothing else. What gives you the right to oppress women? Your strength? Your talents? Consider God's wisdom. Look at the magnificence of the natural world. Doesn't everyone want to live in harmony with nature? Show me, if you can, an example of total male domination in the natural world. Take a look at the animals, study plants, take note of all the different species of life and accept the evidence in front of you. Look really carefully and try to find an instance in nature of the sexes working separately. Everywhere the sexes are interconnected. They co-operate throughout the natural world.

In the whole of nature, only men have claimed dominance as a fundamental truth. In spite of this century of enlightenment and wisdom, man has simply become blind and bloated with science, degenerating into complete ignorance. He wants to control women absolutely even though they are his intellectual equals. He pretends to support the French revolution and the right to equality, simply to avoid any further discussion.

Preamble

Mothers, daughters, sisters - female representatives of the nation - we demand a place in the National Assembly. Women believe that contempt for women's rights is the principal cause of social injustice and corruption in government. Accordingly, women have decided to make a solemn declaration of the natural and inalienable rights of women so that public knowledge of this declaration will remind all members of society of their rights and obligations. Now, when men and women exercise power, their actions can be checked against the aims of their political institutions and they can be held to account. And from now on, society's expectations will be based on simple and self-evident principles so that they will always support the constitution, an equitable society, and the happiness of all.

Women are more beautiful than men. Similarly, women have more courage than men when faced with the pain of childbirth. Women recognise and declare, in the presence of God, the following Rights of Women and of Female Citizens.

Article 1

All women are born free and have equal rights with men. Merit in society should be based solely on the usefulness of an individual's contribution.

Article 2

The purpose of any political body should be to uphold the natural and inalienable rights of women and men. These rights are liberty, property, security and most importantly the right to resist oppression.

Article 3

Authority rests with the nation and the nation is nothing other than its women and men. No body and no individual can exercise any authority that does not come expressly from the nation.

Article 4

Liberty and justice consist of giving to others what rightfully belongs to them. It follows, then, that the only limits on the rights of women are the result of men's continuing oppression. It is only reasonable and natural that these limits should be removed.

Article 5

It is only reasonable and natural to forbid all acts that are harmful to society. Everything else, so long as it is not unreasonable or unnatural, can be permitted. By the same token, no one can be forced to do anything unreasonable and unnatural.

Article 6

The law must express the will of the majority. Men and women must contribute equally to law-making, either personally or through elected representatives. The law must be the same for everyone. Men and women are equal before the law. All titles, positions and public employment must be equally open to both men and women according to their abilities. All appointments should be based solely on merit.

Article 7

No exceptions should be made on account of gender. Women must be accused, arrested and detained as the law determines. All women, like all men, are subject to the law.

Article 8

The law must only set penalties that are strictly and self-evidently appropriate to the crime.

Article 9

When any woman has been found guilty, full and due process of law must take place.

Article 10

No one should be intimidated for expressing their opinions. A woman has the right to mount the scaffold to be hanged. She must equally have the right to mount the speaker's platform to be heard, provided she does not incite people to violence.

Article 11

Freedom of speech is one of a woman's most precious rights because it enables her to name the father of her children. Any woman should be able to say 'you are the father of my child' without having to hide the truth because of social prejudice. But where the law determines that this right has been abused, an exception to this article can be made.

Article 12

Granting and guaranteeing women's rights confers significant benefits: therefore rights must be granted to all women and not just for the benefit of a privileged few.

Article 13

Women and men must contribute equally to the upkeep of the forces of law and order and to the costs of administration: women share the work and the responsibility equally; they should therefore have an equal share of positions, employment, honours and professions.

Article 14

Female and male citizens have the right to determine public spending, either themselves or through their representatives. This can only apply meaningfully to women if they have an equal share of wealth, and an equal influence in public administration, and an equal hand in deciding the proportion, the base, the collection, and the duration of tax.

Article 15

All tax payers - women and men collectively - have the right to demand that any public servant accounts for his actions.

Article 16

No society can have a meaningful constitution without guaranteeing citizens' rights. It is also essential to separate rights from power. The constitution is invalid if the majority that make up the nation have not taken part in drafting it.

Article 17

Property belongs to both sexes, whether together or separate. For each sex, ownership of property is an inviolable right. No one can be deprived of this right unless it has been determined by law that the public good requires it and fair compensation has been agreed in advance.

Postscript

Women, wake up! The alarm bell of reason is ringing throughout the universe. Recognise your rights. The truth is no longer obscured by prejudice, fanaticism, superstition, or lies. Truth has dispelled confusion and oppression. Pre-revolution man was enslaved. He had to increase his power and call on the power of women in order to break his chains through revolutionary action. Once free, he again became unjust to women. Oh, women! When will you open your eyes? What advantages have you gained from the revolution? Greater contempt, even more disrespect. During the centuries of corruption before the revolution, you reigned only over the weakness of men. Now that men are free and strong and that reign is over: what is left to you? The realisation that men are fundamentally unjust? Reclaim your heritage, reclaim your rights based on the natural order of things; what is there to be afraid of in pursuing such a just cause? Our French legislators enforce a moral code long dictated by politics and now out of date. Are you afraid that they will simply say again: how are men and women equal? What have they got in common? Everything, you must reply. If they keep pursuing these irrational trains of thought, contradicting their own post-revolutionary principles, oppose their claims to superiority courageously. Unite with philosophical truth on your side. Use the full force of your character and these superior men, rather than acting as your obedient admirers, will be proud to share with you all the gifts of God. Whatever barriers are thrown in your way, you have the power to overcome them. You simply have to want to.

Let us move on and reflect on the frightful position that women have held in society. Given that a system of national education is now being contemplated, let us see if our legislators will be wise and rational enough to consider the education of women. Women have done more harm than good to their own cause. They have had to live lives full of constraint and they have had to conceal their real feelings. What was taken from them by force, they got back by trickery. They used the power of their feminine wiles and even the most honourable man could not resist. A woman's wiles were more powerful than poison or the sword. Her charms were used just as easily for good or evil. The French government, in particular, depended for centuries on the illicit services of women - secrets were revealed in the indiscretion of the bedroom. Ambassadors, officers, ministers, presidents, pontiffs, and cardinals were all equally susceptible to gold-diggers, and women ambitious for power. Before the revolution, women were despicable yet respected. Post revolution they are respected and despised.

What an opportunity these contradictions offer me for commentary! I have only a moment to make it known but the moment will fix the attention of generations to come. Under the ancien régime[19] everything was deceitful, everything was shameful, yet in spite of this, there were also advantages for women. A woman had only to be beautiful and charming. If she was both, men would lay a hundred fortunes at her feet. If she did not take advantage of them she was regarded as odd or with a bizarre quirk of character that left her unimpressed by wealth. Then she was considered merely awkward. The most indecent woman became respectable through acquiring wealth. The buying of women's favours was a type of trade accepted in the highest social circles. But from now on, it will no longer be acceptable. If it were still acceptable then the revolution would have been a failure and the new relations between men and women would still be corrupt. If a woman has been purchased by a man, is it reasonable to claim that she has no other way of making money, like a slave from the African coast? The difference is enormous. In the case of women, the slave commands the master. But what if the master frees the slave when she is old and has lost her appeal? And what if he gives her no compensation? Then what becomes of this unfortunate woman? She becomes an object of contempt. Even her friends will not help her. They will say she is poor and old, why didn't she make a fortune while she had the chance? Other, even more touching examples come to mind. A young inexperienced woman, seduced by the man she loves, will abandon her parents to follow him. After a few years, he will abandon her. The longer she has been with him the more cruel the betrayal will be. If she has children, he will abandon her anyway. If he is rich, he will consider himself exempt from any obligation to share his fortune with her or her children. Even if some agreement exists requiring him to care for the woman and children, he will ignore it, confident that the law will let him off. If he is married, any other legal agreement is worthless. What law could be made to eradicate faithlessness, injustice and cruelty? One that will share wealth, and public administration, equally between men and women! A woman from a rich family obviously stands to gain a great deal if wealth is shared equally between the male and female members of the family. But what about a woman born into a poor family? Even if she is a good woman, what can she expect? Poverty and disgrace. Unless she excels particularly in music or painting, there's no other position she can hold in public even though she has all the capabilities to do so. I only want to give an overview of how things stand. I will go into more detail in the new edition of my political works that I plan to publish in a few days' time, with notes.

Returning to the subject of morality, marriage is the tomb of trust and love. A married woman can easily have an illegitimate child without her husband realising the child is not his own. She can ensure the child benefits from her husband's wealth even though the child has no rightful claim. An unmarried woman has hardly any rights at all: ancient and inhuman legislation denies her the right to the name or wealth of the father of her children. No post-revolutionary legislation has yet been made to address this situation. Perhaps it seems paradoxical for me to try to ensure women are treated justly and consistently. Perhaps it seems as if I am attempting the impossible. If this is the case, then I leave it to men to find the solution and get the recognition for it. But while we wait, we can prepare the way through national education, restoring morality, and by revising the rules of marriage.

FRAME FOR A SOCIAL CONTRACT BETWEEN MAN AND WOMAN

Olympe de Gouges, 1791

We, N— and N—, joining together for our whole lives by our own free will, and for as long as we are both in love, agree to the following conditions: we intend and wish to combine our assets on condition that they can be divided between our children, and any illegitimate children we may have. We both recognise that our wealth belongs to our children, directly, whatever their origins, and that all our children, without discrimination, have the right to carry the names of the father and mother who have recognised them. We welcome the law that punishes parents who renounce their own offspring. Equally, if we separate, we will share our wealth between us, having deducted our children's share as required by the law. In the case of a perfect, lifelong union, the first to die will give half their assets to their children; if one of the couple were to die childless the other would inherit their wealth unless the deceased bequeathed half their common assets to another person thought appropriate by the deceased.

Here, more or less, is the form of the marriage contract I propose. As this bizarre contract is read, I see rising up against me the hypocrites, the prudes, the clergy, that whole infernal gang. But how many sound ideas the contract offers people wise enough to listen, ideas that will help create better laws and better marriages! I will offer concrete proof in a few words. A rich man with no children will often sleep with a poorer man's wife resulting in the birth of an illegitimate child. When the law enables the poor man's wife to require the rich man to adopt his offspring, the ties of society will be strengthened and morals cleaned up.

This law might protect the good of the community and prevent the breakdown of society where currently many victims become outcasts and their lives degenerate into chaos and suffering.

People who oppose this law should stop complaining about society's immorality or go back to reading the Bible.

I would like a further law to benefit widows and young women cheated by the false promises of men they have become fond of. I would like this law to force fickle lovers to honour their commitments, or to oblige them to pay an indemnity in direct proportion to their wealth. In addition, I would like this law to be rigorously applied to women too where they are offenders and their offence can be proved. As I suggested in *The Primitive Happiness of Man* in 1788, I would also like streetwalkers to be housed in designated areas. It is not streetwalkers who contribute the most to the depravity of morals, it is society women. Housing streetwalkers and giving them a degree of respectability will also improve the behaviour of society women. The bond between them will create disorder at first but will eventually produce a harmonious ensemble.

I suggest a guaranteed method of elevating women: let them have access to the same opportunities as men. If men find this idea impossible, then they must share their wealth with women according to the law rather than their own whims. Prejudice will decrease, morals will improve and equal rights will be established. If priests are also allowed to marry,[20] the King's position will be strengthened and the French government will no longer be in a position to fail.

It's important to say a few words about the trouble I have allegedly caused by asking for better treatment of black men in the French colonies. Cruelty to one's fellow man is unnatural. Some people are so hardened to slavery that they are not touched by rational arguments or appeals to their humanity. Division and discord have caused unrest in the colonies. It is not hard to see who's stirring up trouble; some of them are in the National Assembly itself; they are stirring up trouble that must eventually spread to America. The Colonists, brothers and fathers of the men they hold as slaves, go against nature and persecute men to whom they are related. These inhuman Colonists say: 'Our blood flows in their veins but we will spill it all, if we must, to hide our greed or our ambition.' It is in the colonies, so close to nature, that fathers disown their sons; they refuse to recognise their descendents and turn their backs on family life. How can this state of affairs be put right? It's a terrible idea to use violence. But to do nothing means the injustice will simply be transported to America. The hand of God seems to protect man's inalienable right to liberty. Only the law has the right to curtail a man's liberty if he uses the idea of liberty as an excuse for bad behaviour. But the law must be the same and must be applied equally to everyone. The law must govern the conduct of the National Assembly and it must be wise and just. The law must act in the same way for the French state and it must pay as much attention to the terrible new abuses as it has to the old.

I am still of the opinion that it is important to reconcile the executive power of the king and the legislative power of parliament. At the moment, it seems to me that one is everything and the other is nothing. Unfortunately, this may cause the collapse of the French Empire. I think executive and legislative power are like a man and a woman who must be united with equal rights if they are to live well together.

No one can escape their destiny. I experienced this today. I had decided that I would not include any humour in this text. But then fate stepped in. Here's what happened:

The economy is not properly regulated and this is even

more true in times of upheaval. I live in the countryside. I left Auteuil this morning at eight and made my way to the road that goes from Paris to Versailles where there's often one of those roadside cafés that's very popular because it's cheap. I was unlucky that morning. I reached the gate and I could not even find the hackney coach. Nine o'clock chimed and I continued on my way. I spotted a coach, took my place, and arrived at a quarter past nine at the Pont-Royal according to two different watches. I took the hackney coach and rushed to my printer in the rue Christine. It was important to get there early because there is always so much to do: the pages are too closely typeset or there is too much type per page or other problems. I stayed about twenty minutes. I felt tired from walking, writing and printing so I decided to go to the baths in the Temple district where I was dining later. I arrived at a quarter to eleven by the clock in the baths. That meant I owed the coachman for an hour and a half but to avoid a fight with him I offered him 48 sous. As usual he demanded more money. I refused to give him more than I owed him. Like any fair person, I don't mind being generous but I won't be made a fool of. I threatened him with the law. He said he didn't care and insisted that I pay him for two hours. We found a justice of the peace. I am not going to name him, although the way he dealt with me merits a formal complaint.

I'm certain he was unaware that the woman asking for justice was the writer of so many works calling for social justice. He ignored my reasons and said I was to pay the coachman what he was asking for. Knowing the law better than he did, I said, 'I refuse and I would also like to point out that you are exceeding your authority.' So this man, or to put it a better way, this lunatic, got carried away and threatened me with prison if I didn't pay up straightaway. He said he would keep me in his office all day. I asked him to take me to the district tribunal, or the town hall, as I was going to make a formal complaint against his abuse of power. The self-important magistrate, whose riding coat was as disgusting as his manners, tells me pleasantly: 'No doubt you'll want to take your complaint to the National Assembly?' 'That may well be,' I said, half furious and half laughing at this modern-day Bride-Oison,[21] 'So this is the type of man who is to judge an enlightened People!' This sort of thing happens all the time. Good people, as well as bad ones, suffer the same kind of injustices. There's only one thing to say about the state of the sections and tribunals: justice is non existant. The law is ignored and, God knows how, the police have just got used to it. It's impossible to find the coachmen who have been looking after your luggage. They change their numbers whenever they like and several people, including myself, have lost their belongings in their vehicles. Under the ancien régime, for all its faults, you could track down your luggage by arranging a roll-call of the coachmen and inspecting their numbers. You could count on that. What are the justices of the peace doing? What are the superintendents doing, the inspectors of the new regime? Nothing at all or feathering their own nests. The National Assembly must pay special attention to this particular group who are supposed to protect society.

P.S. This work was written in a few days. It was delayed at the press and was already being printed when M. Talleyrand[22], whose name will always be famous, published his work on the principles of national education. I am very happy to say I agree with his views! In the meantime, I had to stop the press and shout with joy when I heard that the king had just accepted the Constitution and that the National Assembly had unanimously proclaimed a general amnesty. Now I love the National Assembly, even Abbé Maury[23] and LaFayette[24] who is a god to me. Please God, let this cause for joy be real. Send back all our fugitives in a great parade so that we can line their route and praise your power on this momentous day.

NOTES

1. For twelve years Inga Beale played as a back row forward for the London Wasps Women's rugby team. She approached professional level, playing as part of the club's first team in the first division. Her rugby days gained her the nickname 'Inga the Winger'.

2. *Remember 1967* is a 2017 artwork by public artist Martin Firrell. The *Remember 1967* series consists of six digital billboards created to mark the 50th anniversary of the Sexual Offences Act 1967. The artworks were displayed nationally on digital billboards throughout the UK in July 2017. With the passing of the 1967 Act, gay and bisexual men in England and Wales were able to have sexual relationships for the first time without being automatically criminalised. *Remember 1967* echoed demands made by activists in the 1960s that still warrant action in the present day.

3. Michael Peschardt is the BBC's Sydney correspondent covering a range of stories from Australia and South East Asia for the BBC's UK-based TV and Radio services. He is a regular contributor to BBC Radio 4, BBC News, and the international channel BBC World News.

4. General Electric Company (GE) is an American multinational conglomerate incorporated in New York City and headquartered in Boston. The Insurance Division is part of GE Capital providing commercial lending and leasing, and a range of financial services for commercial aviation, energy and GE's industrial business units.

5. An insurance company credit rating is the opinion of an independent agency regarding the financial strength of an insurance company. An insurance company's credit rating indicates its ability to pay policyholders' claims. It does not indicate how well the insurance company's securities are performing for investors. In addition, an insurance company's credit rating is considered an opinion, not a fact, and ratings of the same insurance company can differ among rating agencies.

6. James Joseph Schiro (2 January 1946 - 13 August 2014) was an American businessman who became CEO of Price Waterhouse Coopers and Zurich Financial Services. He was also a director of several multinational companies including Pepsico, Philips and Goldman Sachs. From 2002 to 2006, Schiro served as the CEO of Zurich Financial Services. He served on the Board of the Geneva Association and was a member of the European Financial Services Roundtable.

7. Antonia Belcher (FRICS, FCABE, FCIARB, and FRSA) is a founding partner of the building consultancy MHBC. Notable project work includes the base builds for Unilever and Coca Cola's HQ, the Royal Courts of Justice and the development of Leicester City FC's Walker Stadium. Since Antonia transitioned in 2000, she has advocated the value of diversity in the workplace. She has been recognised as one of the Financial Times' Top 100 LGBT+ Executives in 2014, 2015, and 2016.

8. In the English-speaking world, the term 'French feminism' refers to a branch of feminist theories and philosophies that emerged in the 1970s. French feminist theory, compared to its English-speaking counterpart, is distinguished by an approach which is more philosophical and literary. Its writings tend to be effusive and metaphorical. Notable representatives include Monique Wittig, Hélène Cixous, Luce Irigaray, Julia Kristeva and Bracha Ettinger. The term includes writers who are not French, but who have worked substantially in France and the French tradition.

9. The Reign of Terror refers to the period during the French revolution immediately after the First French Republic was established. Several historians consider the Reign of Terror to have begun in 1793, placing the starting date at either 5 September, June or March. Others consider it to have begun in September 1792 or even July 1789 (when the first lynchings took place). There is a consensus that it ended with the fall of Maximilien Robespierre in July 1794. Between June 1793 and July 1794, there were 16,594 official death sentences in France, of which 2,639 were in Paris.

10. The Girondists were members of a loosely knit political faction during the French revolution. From 1791 to 1793, the Girondins were active in the Legislative Assembly and the National Convention, campaigning for the abolition of the monarchy.

11. The Comédie-Française is one of the few state theatres in France. Founded in 1680, it is considered the oldest active theatre company in the world. The company's primary venue is the Salle Richelieu, which is a part of the Palais-Royal complex in the 1st arrondissement of Paris.

12. Abraham Joseph Bénard aka Fleury (26 October 1750 - 3 March 1822) was a French actor of the Comédie-Française and one of the greatest comedians of his time. He was arrested in 1793, during the French revolution, for appearing in the controversial play *L' Ami des lois* (*The Friend of Laws*) by the French playwright Jean-Louis Laya (4 December 1761 - 25 August 1833). The play protested against mob rule with scarcely veiled characterisations of Robespierre and Marat.

13. The Society of the Friends of Truth (Amis de la Verité), also known as the Social Club (Cercle Social), was a French revolutionary organisation founded in 1790. It was a mixture of revolutionary political club, the Masonic Lodge, and a literary salon. It also published an influential revolutionary newspaper, *The Mouth of Iron*.

14. Sophie de Condorcet (1764 - 8 September 1822) was a prominent salon hostess from 1789 until the Reign of Terror, and again from 1799 until her death in 1822. She was the wife, then widow, of the mathematician and philosopher Nicolas de Condorcet. Despite his death, and the exile of her brother Marshal Emmanuel, Marquis de Grouchy between 1815 and 1821, she maintained her own identity and was well connected and influential before, during, and after the French revolution. Unlike her fellow Girondist hostess, Madame Roland, Madame de Condorcet included other women in her salons, notably Olympe de Gouges. De Condorcet was also a writer and a translator in her own right, highly educated for her day, and fluent in

English and Italian. She produced influential translations of Thomas Paine and Adam Smith.

15. A Jacobin was a member of the Jacobin Club, a revolutionary political movement and the most famous political club during the French revolution (1789 - 1799). The club was named after the Dominican convent in Paris where its members originally met. The Jacobins supported a centralised republican state and extensive government intervention to transform society.

16. L'église de la Madeleine or La Madeleine is a Roman Catholic church occupying a commanding position in the 8th arrondissement of Paris. The Madeleine Church was designed in its present form as a temple to the glory of Napoleon's army. To its south lies the Place de la Concorde, to the east is the Place Vendôme, and to the west Saint-Augustin, Paris.

17. The Furies of the Guillotine were women who attended the public executions of the French revolution. Between beheadings, they knitted. These tricoteuse, or knitting women, became friendly with the executioners and were regarded at first as respected sisters of the resistance.

18. Marie Antoinette (2 November 1755 - 16 October 1793) was the last Queen of France. She was born an Archduchess of Austria and was the penultimate child and youngest daughter of Empress Maria Theresa and Francis I, Holy Roman Emperor. She became Dauphine of France in May 1770 at age 14 when she was married to Louis-Auguste, heir apparent to the French throne. On 10 May 1774, her husband ascended the throne as Louis XVI and she assumed the title Queen of France and Navarre, which she held until September 1791. She then became Queen of the French as the French revolution proceeded, a title that she held until 21 September 1792.

19. The ancien régime or 'old regime' was the political and social system of the Kingdom of France from the Late Middle Ages

(c.1400) until 1789 when hereditary monarchy and the feudal system of French nobility were abolished by the French revolution.

20. During the French revolution, priests were encouraged to marry in three waves of reform and disruption of the Catholic Church. From the beginning of 1791 to September 1793 priests were free to choose to marry, and 8% did so. From October 1793 to the end of 1794 revolutionaries tried to eradicate the Constitutional Church and its clergy by forcing them to marry. This period is called the 'Dechristianisation of year II' and nearly 70% of priests married at the time. From the beginning of 1795 to June 1815, 22% of priests married. These marriages were once again by choice. Some priests married to put into practice Enlightenment principles becoming 'citizen priests' but most who married before the Fall of 1793 did so as a rejection of their vocation.

21. Don Guzman Brid'oison, a judge, is a character in the French play the Marriage of Figaro by Pierre-Augustin Caron de Beaumarchais (1732 - 1799). The term 'Brid'oison now refers to anyone with a love of red tape.

22. Charles-Maurice de Talleyrand-Périgord (2 February 1754 - 17 May 1838), 1st Prince of Benevento, then 1st Duke of Talleyrand, was a French politician and diplomat. In 1780 he was appointed Agent-General of the Clergy and represented the Catholic Church to the French Crown. He worked at the highest levels of successive French governments. On 10 September 1791, in the closing days of the Constituent Assembly, Talleyrand outlined his ideas on national education. Education was to be free, and to lead to attendance at university. In place of dogma, the elements of religion were alone to be taught.

23. Jean-Sifrein Maury (26 June 1746 - 10 May 1817) was a French cardinal, archbishop of Paris, and former bishop of Montefiascone. Famous for immorality but also wit. In the National Constituent Assembly he took an active part in every important debate, in particular opposing the confiscation of property held by the clergy.

24. Marie-Joseph Paul Yves Roch Gilbert du Motier, Marquis de
    Lafayette (6 September 1757 - 20 May 1834), known in the United
    States simply as Lafayette, was a French aristocrat and military
    officer who fought in the American Revolutionary War, commanding
    American troops in several battles. On his return to France, he
    became a key figure in the French revolution of 1789. After forming
    the National Constituent Assembly, he helped to write the
    Declaration of the Rights of Man and of the Citizen with Thomas
    Jefferson's assistance. This document was inspired by the United
    States Declaration of Independence and invoked natural law to
    establish basic principles of the democratic nation-state. He also
    advocated the end of slavery, in keeping with the philosophy of
    natural liberty.

MARTIN FIRRELL

The public artist Martin Firrell uses text in public space to promote debate. The more people think about, question and debate a topic, the more likely it becomes that change will occur.

Firrell uses language to engage directly with the public, promoting constructive dialogues, usually about marginalisation, equality and more equitable social organisation, with the aim of making the world more humane. His work has been summarised as 'art as debate'.

Socialart.work is a mass public art project created by Martin Firrell calling for greater social justice. It aims to create debate about power and its abuse, feminism, women's equality and gender, alternative forms of economic and social organisation, black power, counter-culture, and solidarity between people of different backgrounds and ethnicities.

The project includes posters, publications and events supported in 2018-19 by the digital media company Clear Channel UK.

Martin Firrell has been described in the Guardian newspaper as 'one of the capital's most influential public artists'.

More information about this project can be found at www.socialart.work. More information about the artist can be found at Wikipedia.

Lightning Source UK Ltd.
Milton Keynes UK
UKHW011655170822
407425UK00004B/298